The New Covenant
and
New Covenant Theology

Two Lectures
Presented at the 2008
John Bunyan Conference
Lewisburg, PA

Fred G. Zaspel

5317 Wye Creek Drive, Frederick, MD 21703-6938
phone: 301-473-8781 or 800-376-4146 fax: 240-206-0373
email: info@newcovenantmedia.com
Website: www.newcovenantmedia.com

The New Covenant
and
New Covenant Theology

Copyright 2011© by Fred G. Zaspel

Published by: New Covenant Media
5317 Wye Creek Drive
Frederick, Maryland 21703-6938

Orders: www.newcovenantmedia.com

Printed in the United States of America

ISBN 13: 978-1-928965-34-3

Table of Contents

The New Covenant

Covenant and Covenants in Scripture

Even the most elementary acquaintance with the Bible recognizes in some degree the prominence of the covenant concept. Not only are there covenants with Noah, Abraham, Israel, and so on, but the most basic division of the biblical material is described in terms of old and new covenants.[1] It really does not take much effort from there to notice that covenant is not only a recurring theme in Scripture, but even a major unifying theme and organizing factor.

By way of definition, I will take the one given by Paul Williamson in his recent and major study on biblical covenants[2]: "a solemn commitment, guaranteeing promises or obligations undertaken by one or both parties, sealed with an oath." And although it has been pointed out by many, we should at least mention here in passing that the covenants of Scripture reflect covenantal structures of the ancient Near East, a historical observation that is sometimes useful in understanding the suzerain-vassal treaties as bilateral or conditional, and the royal grant treaties as unilateral and unconditional.

---

[1] E.g., Hebrews 8:6-10.

[2] Paul R. Williamson, Sealed with an Oath: Covenant in God's Unfolding Purpose (Downers Grove, IL: IVP; New Studies in Biblical Theology series, D.A. Carson, ed.), p. 11.

As Williamson and others have pointed out, the biblical covenants were each given successively to advance God's redemptive purpose.

- In the Noahic covenant, God guarantees the continued future of the created order despite the depths of human rebellion, curse, and judgment that seemed to have threatened it.

- In the Abrahamic covenant, God promises a seed, a land, and blessing to Abraham personally, nationally, and internationally—a promise that advances and secures the fulfillment of the Noahic covenant.

- In the Mosaic or Sinaitic covenant, God sets out the covenantal obligations for those of ethnic and national descent from Abraham. Israel is to mediate blessing to the surrounding nations by modeling the kingdom of God on earth and living according to her covenant law. This covenant ultimately failed as Israel did not fulfill her obligations, seemingly jeopardizing the fulfillment of God's international agenda.

- The Davidic covenant guarantees the royal seed promised to Abraham who would successfully secure the blessings in both the national and international aspects of God's gracious purpose.

- Finally, the new covenant promises to overcome the failure of the sinful people with whom the covenant is made. Their failure will not interfere with the successful accomplishment of God's purpose, but God will make provision both for failure and for eventual faithfulness, and he will secure eternal fellowship with his people.

The biblical covenants, then, take us from ruin to redemption and outline in broad strokes the purpose of God in human history. Of course, all of this is the outworking of the larger promise theme first introduced in Genesis 3:15 (whether this is itself, properly speaking, a "covenant" promise is a topic for another occasion). Moreover, all of this, including Genesis 3:15, is the unfolding of a promise which according to Titus 1:2 was made before time began. It would be difficult to find a larger and more unifying theme running all through scripture than the theme of promise.

Sometimes this theme is highlighted by the word "promise" itself, but more often it is simply the ordinary language of God "saying," "speaking," "swearing," or "making an oath" to his chosen people. Sometimes this promise is solemnized in a formal covenant. And within this larger framework, the new covenant appears at the climax. It is not only chronologically last, but it is the fullest and most comprehensive. It is held out as Israel's hope in an array of Old Testament passages—once under the name "new covenant" (Jer. 31:34), seven times as an "everlasting covenant" (Jer. 32-33 [cf. 32:40]; 50:5; Ezek. 16:60; 37:26; Isa. 24:5; 55:3; 61:8; cf. Hos. 2:14-23), three times as the "covenant of peace" (Isa. 54:10; Ezek. 34:25; 37:26), sometimes with no specific "covenant" name attached at all (Ezek. 36:22ff), and once the Servant of the Lord is said himself to be the covenant (Isa. 49:8). And in these passages and more, this new covenant takes up into itself promises made centuries before in covenants with Noah, Abraham, Moses, and Israel. This is the covenant the Lord Jesus ratified in his own blood, and it is not without reason that the entire back half of our Bibles very early came to be designated "the new covenant" or "the new testament." It is not surprising that Jeremiah 31:31-34, the prophecy of the new covenant, is the longest single Old Testament quotation found in the New Testament—twice quoted at length within the space of three chapters (Heb. 8:8-12 and 10:16-17). Even without direct quotation of the related Old Testament passages, the new covenant is the subject of discussion in at least nine other New Testament passages (Luke 22:20; 1 Cor. 11:25; Matt. 26:28; Mark 14:24 [Lord's Supper passages]; also Rom. 11:27; 2 Cor. 3:6; Heb. 9:15; 10:13; 12:24). Again, even within this larger context of promise and covenant, the new covenant is a major biblical theme indeed.

Exposition of the New Covenant

Jeremiah 31:31-34 is considered *the* Old Testament passage on the new covenant because it is the only passage that uses the specific language "new covenant," because it is the fullest statement of that covenant in all the prophets, and because it is the passage the New Testament writers most often cited in discussion of this covenant (Matt. 26:28; Mark 14:24; Luke 22:20; Eph. 2:11-12; Heb. 8:8-12; 10:16-17). But the new covenant promise is the topic of prophetic hope in other passages also, such as Isaiah 59:20-21, Jeremiah 32:37-40, and Ezekiel 16:60-63 and 37:21-28. We will take Jeremiah 31:31-34 as our primary point of reference while trying to keep an eye on the related passages.

Jeremiah 31:27-40:

> "The days are coming," declares the LORD, "when I will plant the house of Israel and the house of Judah with the off-spring of men and of animals. Just as I watched over them to uproot and tear down, and to overthrow, destroy and bring

disaster, so I will watch over them to build and to plant," de-
clares the LORD. "In those days people will no longer say, 'The
fathers have eaten sour grapes, and the children's teeth are set
on edge.' Instead, everyone will die for his own sin; whoever
eats sour grapes – his own teeth will be set on edge. "The time
is coming," declares the LORD, "when I will make a new cove-
nant with the house of Israel and with the house of Judah. It
will not be like the covenant I made with their forefathers when
I took them by the hand to lead them out of Egypt, because they
broke my covenant, though I was a husband to them," declares
the LORD. "This is the covenant I will make with the house of
Israel after that time," declares the LORD. "I will put my law
in their minds and write it on their hearts. I will be their God,
and they will be my people. No longer will a man teach his
neighbor, or a man his brother, saying, 'Know the LORD,' be-
cause they will all know me, from the least of them to the great-
est," declares the LORD. "For I will forgive their wickedness
and will remember their sins no more." This is what the LORD
says, he who appoints the sun to shine by day, who decrees the
moon and stars to shine by night, who stirs up the sea so that
its waves roar – the LORD Almighty is his name: "Only if these
decrees vanish from my sight," declares the LORD, "will the de-
scendants of Israel ever cease to be a nation before me." This is
what the LORD says: "Only if the heavens above can be meas-
ured and the foundations of the earth below be searched out
will I reject all the descendants of Israel because of all they have
done," declares the LORD. "The days are coming," declares the
LORD, "when this city will be rebuilt for me from the Tower of
Hananel to the Corner Gate. The measuring line will stretch
from there straight to the hill of Gareb and then turn to Goah.
The whole valley where dead bodies and ashes are thrown, and
all the terraces out to the Kidron Valley on the east as far as the
corner of the Horse Gate, will be holy to the LORD. The city
will never again be uprooted or demolished."

Context

At the outset of his ministry, Jeremiah was told by the Lord that in his role as prophet he was called "to uproot and tear down, to destroy and overthrow, to build and to plant" (Jer. 1:10). Accordingly, his message was one of both judgment and hope. Chapters 30-33 of his prophecy focus on the latter and are commonly known as "the book of comfort," "the book of consolation," or "the book of hope." Throughout the years prior to Israel's exile, Jeremiah warned and denounced the nation for her backsliding and turning away from the Lord God. He rebuked governmental officials, prophets, and people alike, and he warned of that coming time of unprecedented trouble for Jacob. But in chapters 30-33 the outlook is one marked by grace, comfort, and hope. God will restore his people to their land (30:3) and raise up the Davidic king (30:9). (Note here the explicit links to the Abrahamic and Davidic covenants.) God will bring salvation to his people (30:10), destroy her oppressors (30:16), and reestablish her in prosperity (30:17ff) and in fellowship with him (30:22). Not because she deserves it, but simply because God loves his people with an everlasting love (31:3), he will bring her again through a new exodus (cf. 30:3, 8, 16-17; 31:9, 12-14) to the place of privilege and blessing.

Structure

Verses 31-34 form the heart of the new covenant prophecy and are the verses quoted in the New Testament by the writer to the Hebrews. The familiar phrase "declares the LORD" routinely sets off the words of the prophet as oracular sayings, and in this case the recurrence of the phrase and the explanatory conjunction "for" (*ki*) serve to outline the passage for us. Notice that the phrase "declares the LORD" (*ne'um yhwh*) occurs four times in these verses—at the beginning of verse 31 and at the end of verse 32, bracketing the first division of the prophecy; then again at the beginning of verse 33 and near the end of verse 34, setting off the second division. Then the prophecy concludes with the final explanatory ("for") clause of verse 34.

The verses then make three major statements.

First—

> 31 *"The time is coming," declares the LORD, "when I will make a new covenant with the house of Israel and with the house of Judah. 32 It will not be like the covenant I made with their forefathers when I took them by the hand to lead them out of Egypt, because they broke my covenant, though I was a husband to them," declares the LORD.*

Second—

> 33 *"This is the covenant I will make with the house of Israel after that time," declares the LORD. "I will put my law in their minds and write it on their hearts. I will be their God, and they will be my people. 34a No longer will a man teach his neighbor, or a man his brother, saying, 'Know the LORD,' because they will all know me, from the least of them to the greatest," declares the LORD.*

Then the climactic explanatory clause—

> 34b *"For I will forgive their wickedness and will remember their sins no more."*

The first statement (vv. 31-32) provides a general introduction, affirming that the new covenant will not be like the old. The second (vv. 33-34) specifies the contents of the new covenant. Then finally, the "for" clause at the end of verse 34 states the foundation or the basis of these promises. We have an introductory statement, providing a general contrast of the new covenant with the old, then a statement of the provisions of the covenant, and then finally an explanation of the ground on which these promises will be given.

Time Frame

Jeremiah's phrase "in those days" (Jer. 31:29; cf. v. 31) is indefinite and can, in Jeremiah and the prophets, often have in view either the near or the distant future, and very often both. The historical context of this prophecy indicates that the prophet is encouraging the people of Israel first in reference to the coming captivity and exile, reminding her that it will not be permanent, but that God will again bring her home from that exile.

However, as is common in biblical prophecy, the language of the prophecy in this context takes us beyond the immediate setting to "the latter days" (30:24). Verse 33 says it will be "after those days," referring evidently to the time of Jacob's trouble (30:7), the time of Israel's chastening, and of her subsequent regathering (chapters 30-31). In his Olivet Discourse, Jesus placed the period of Jacob's trouble in a time frame that was future to him (Matt. 24:21), and in Romans 11:26-27 Paul specifically refers this prophecy to the time of Christ's return. Once more, in Jeremiah 33:15-16, the prophet describes this time as marked by the reign of the Davidic king par excellence, "the righteous Branch," over his people in peace and safety. It is not our purpose to enter discussions of eschatology here, but it should be noted at the outset that Jeremiah is painting with broad strokes, and we should expect to see in this covenant promise not only the enacting, but also the unfolding and final fulfillment of God's comprehensive redemptive purpose.

Parties

Who is addressed in these prophecies? And who is to receive the promised blessings? Dispensational theology lays stress on the nation of Israel, who is clearly the people addressed when the prophecy is given, while Reformed theology lays stress on the church as the fulfiller of these promises. Thankfully, there is in recent years among both dispensational and Reformed theologians an increasing consensus on some of the previously debated issues involved in the study of this and related covenants. From the dispensational side there has been a concession that "Abraham's seed" is a term that includes not only ethnic Israel but ultimately believing Jews and Gentiles in Christ, the church. And from the Reformed side, especially since John Murray's commentary on Romans, there has been increasing agreement that the ancient promises do indeed extend specific hope for ethnic Israel. Older dispensational and Reformed theologians fought tooth and nail over these matters. Some from the dispensationalist side went so far as to argue for *two* new covenants—one for Israel and then another for the church—and some would deny any relevance of Old Testament kingdom prophecies to the church age. Reformed theologians, on the other hand, often would simply replace Israel with the church—leave Israel with her covenanted curses and transfer her covenanted promises to the church, and that was that. Both approaches had obvious problems. Today, happily, less is heard from either extreme, and so both sides can say they have won—at least a little. Many differences remain, of course, but a good deal of common ground has been found.

So also in this new covenant prophecy there can be little doubt that the promise is made with ethnic Israel. This is its stated and exclusive emphasis in virtually all of its leading statements (e.g., Jer. 30-32; Ezek. 34; 36; 37). Yet if, as seems obvious, the new covenant takes up into it the strands of promise given earlier in the Abrahamic and Davidic covenants (e.g., Ezek. 16:60-63; 34:23-31), it would be surprising if it did not culminate in Gentile blessing also. Still given the specific and emphatic statements of the covenant, it would be more surprising still to find that Israel has been left out altogether. And, in fact, this "both/and" direction is what is taken in the New Testament. To borrow Paul's analogy, the wild branches have been grafted into the same Abrahamic tree to live together with the natural branches, and in this one people of God, the church, Jew and Gentile together enjoy the realization of the ancient promises. The new covenant enacted in Christ's blood is *the* covenant of the Christian church comprising all believers, Jew and Gentile alike, in which the ancient promises are finally realized. The inclusion of the church in the provisions of the new covenant made with Israel is the explicit teaching of 2 Corinthians 3, Ephesians 2:11-20, and Hebrews 8-10 and is reflected clearly in Matthew 26:28, Mark 14:24, and Luke 22:20 where our Lord memorializes the new covenant promise of forgiveness in the church ordinance of the Lord's supper.

Walter Kaiser makes the analogy of the excitement of being included in an invitation we did not expect. In a way similar to this, we Gentiles should rejoice in our inclusion in this covenant. We who were foreigners and had no covenant at all have been brought in to enjoy these blessings promised first for others.[3] Albert Baylis has described the situation in terms of a corporate executive who owns two separate companies. When the one company unionized, the owner, without obligation but out of the goodness of his heart, extended the same benefits to his other non-union company also.[4] Likewise, Gentiles have been brought to partake of Israel's covenant promises also, and in the church both enjoy the new covenant blessings together.

This discussion of Israel and the church and the parties of the covenant inevitably leads to questions of future eschatology, but since this is not the focus of our attention here we will not pursue this subject further. Suffice it to say at this point that the same apostle Paul who relates this covenant to the church in 2 Corinthians 3 also cites it in Romans 11:26-27 as ground for his hope for the future redemption of Israel when the Deliverer comes from Zion. The issue here is clearly one of "both/and," but the attending eschatological details will have to be left for another time.

Provisions of the New Covenant

Restoration of Israel to her Land In the new covenant prophecies great stress is laid on the restoration of Israel to her land and the steps God will take to ensure her faithfulness.

---

[3] Walter C. Kaiser, Jr., "Included in the Covenant," (*Moody Monthly:* June 1991), p. 34.

[4] Albert H. Baylis, *On the Way to Jesus.* (Portland, OR: Multnomah Press, 1986), pp. 298-9.

Jeremiah 31:27-28: "The days are coming, declares the LORD, when I will plant the house of Israel and the house of Judah with the offspring of men and of animals. Just as I watched over them to uproot and tear down, and to overthrow, destroy and bring disaster, so I will watch over them to build and to plant, declares the LORD."

Ezekiel 36:22-24, 28: "Therefore say to the house of Israel, This is what the Sovereign LORD says: It is not for your sake, O house of Israel, that I am going to do these things, but for the sake of my holy name, which you have profaned among the nations where you have gone. I will show the holiness of my great name, which has been profaned among the nations, the name you have profaned among them. Then the nations will know that I am the LORD, declares the Sovereign LORD, when I show myself holy through you before their eyes. For I will take you out of the nations; I will gather you from all the countries and bring you back into your own land.... You will live in the land I gave your forefathers."

Similar assurances are given in Ezekiel 34:25-31, 37:21-28, and Jeremiah 32:37-40. And this theme figures prominently throughout Jeremiah's Book of Comfort in which this prophecy is given (see Jer. 31:8-16, 23; 32:40-41). But the promise that the new covenant prophets hold out to Israel is not merely restoration to the land , but restoration in safety and without war (see for example Jer. 32:37; Ezek. 28:25; 34:25-31; 38:8-11; Hos. 2:18; Zech. 14:11; cf. Luke 1:67-75; Rom. 4:13). Again, this discussion is not specific to our focus here and need not detain us. Of greatest importance is the emphasis that her restoration will be salvific, and to this we will give the remainder of our attention.

Soteric Restoration

1. Law Written on the Heart

The soteriologically redemptive provisions of the covenant are underlined by Jesus and the New Testament writers in referencing this covenant to the church. First, God says, "I will put my law in their inward parts, and write it in their hearts" (Jer. 31:33). That is, his law will be internalized. The failure of the old law was in large part due to the fact that its demands were only external, written on stones. There was nothing about it that supplied the motivation for compliance, nothing to effect desire. But under this covenant God, in grace, will so change his people—each of them, individually—that their obedience will come as a matter of course. In Adam the human heart is naturally bent toward rebellion, but under this covenant that will be changed, and God's people will be transformed and be given a mind and heart to obey. Ezekiel elaborates in still more graphic terms: "I will give you a new heart and put a new spirit in you; I will remove from you your heart of stone and give you a heart of flesh. And I will put my Spirit in you and move you to follow my decrees and be careful to keep my laws" (Ezek. 36:26-27). Clearly, the emphasis here is on moral transformation. God will renew his people so that their hearts will no longer be like stone—hard and unimpressionable—but pliable like flesh and moldable to conform to God's will. God will accomplish this by the powerful workings of his Spirit now given to dwell within. God himself will lead and move his people upward to conform to that moral ideal to which they were called. In short, God will do for them and in them what he requires of them. He will bring his people to experienced godliness by powerfully transforming them from within. Caught up in all this, of course, are the doctrines of regeneration, sanctification, perseverance (cf. Jer. 32:40), and even glorification.

We should clarify briefly that this is not to imply that old covenant believers did not experience regeneration or that the Spirit of God was inactive during that time in terms of his inward transforming work. It is to say, merely, that these soteric blessings were not provided *under the terms of* the old covenant as they are under the terms of the new covenant. We will return to this point in due course.

Some Reformed interpreters have stressed that the phrase "writing God's law on the heart" refers to content rather than will or desire and motivation. Specifically, it is important for them to preserve the special status of the Decalogue as the eternal and unchanging moral law of God, and so the argument is made that it is this, the Ten Commandments, that God etches on the heart.

It would be difficult to deny that the expression has some reference to content, but neither can it be denied that the prophecy, in its expressions both by Jeremiah and Ezekiel, lays specific stress on inward transformation of heart and mind and will, a replacing of a stony heart with a heart of flesh and with the impartation of God's Spirit. The stress is plainly on renewal, inward transformation, and a newly caused willingness to obey. The failure of the old covenant was not due to a lack of awareness (content) but a lack of heart to do God's will. This was Moses' own word of rebuke to Israel on the plains of Moab. This—the want of a heart to follow God—was the cause of their exile to the wilderness, and now it was the cause of their exile to Babylon. But it is this problem of an unresponsive heart to God that God now promises to correct.

Still, it is difficult to think of all this willingness to obey God's law apart from some understanding of what that law demands (content). So what exactly is the content of this law now written on the heart? Is it the Decalogue? What is the shape of God's law under the new covenant? Certainly one would expect an extensive degree of continuity between the law of the old covenant and that of the new, for it is, after all, the same God who stands behind both covenants and issues "his law" to both covenant communities. Of course this proves to be the case, as even a quick reading of the Old and New Testaments will reveal.

Even so, to identify "my law" with the Decalogue seems overly reductionistic, and Jeremiah's prophecy does not require such an absolute identification. He simply looks forward to a time when God will again give "his law" under the terms of a new and different covenant. Indeed, he speaks in terms of disjunction, even replacement, and explicitly states that this new covenant will be "not like" the old. In determining the content of this promised law to be written on the heart, it is better, with Williamson, to understand the expression as "summarizing the essence of God's Torah, as reflected in the Mosaic law and throughout Scripture." This seems to be the direction von Orelli takes.[5] The specific demands this promised "law written on the heart" will entail can then only be defined by an examination of the covenant of which that law is a part. Most help-

---

[5] C. von Orelli, *The Prophecies of Jeremiah,* trans. J.S. Banks (1889; reprint, Minneapolis: Klock and Klock, 1977), p. 241.

fully, Doug Moo argues that "God's law" is no longer binding in its old covenant form but in the new form it is given
in Christ. We will see this again in the next lecture.[6]

Moreover, it would seem that Jeremiah's prophecy at
this point reflects the expectation, born in Deuteronomy
18:15-18, of a new prophet and lawgiver to come. This
prophet to come would, like Moses, bring God's law to his
people, and they would be responsible to God to obey the
law he brings. This expectation is echoed, for instance, in
Isaiah 42:4 where the coast lands of the world are portrayed as waiting for the Servant of the Lord to bring God's
law (torato) to them (cf. Isa. 2:3; 51:4; Mic. 4:2). Such expressions seem to imply a degree of newness, not simply dupli-
cation. And, of course, this expectation finds its realization
in Christ, who in his earthly ministry spoke with the Father's authorization (Matt. 17:5) and insisted, on threat of
condemnation, that his word be obeyed (Matt. 7:21-29; cf.
John 17:8). If we are pressed to find a precise answer to this
part of Jeremiah's prophecy, it would seem easiest to find it
not in the Decalogue but here—the law which the coming
lawgiver will bring. We will visit this matter again in the
following lecture.

Once again, although it would be impossible to miss the
idea of God's law having recognizable content, Jeremiah
and Ezekiel clearly emphasize inward transformation resulting in willing and inevitable compliance. The old cove-

---

[6] Douglas J. Moo, "The Law of Christ as the Fulfillment of the Law of
    Moses: A Modified Lutheran View," in Five Views on Law and Gospel,
    ed. Stanley N. Gundry (Grand Rapids: Zondervan, 1996), pp. 310-
    82.

nant failed because it could not ensure obedience to its terms on the part of the people. Under the new covenant things will be very different. God's people—each of them individually—will be given a mind and a heart to love and serve their God; they will loathe their former sins (Ezek. 36:31), turn to God, and follow him faithfully with all their heart.

2. The Presence and Knowledge of God

The second redemptive provision of the new covenant is the promise, "I will be their God, and they will be my people" (Jer. 31:33). This seems to connote the idea of relationship and fellowship, and this is the direction God takes it in the next breath: "No longer will a man teach his neighbor, or a man his brother, saying, Know the LORD, because they will all know me, from the least of them to the greatest, declares the LORD" (31:34). The idea of salvific fellowship with God (reconciliation) is obvious.

If any passage declares plainly that the old covenant community was not a soteriologically redeemed people, it is this one. Not everyone in that covenant community knew God, and so prophets were sent to urge the people to know him and to call them to him in repentance. Of course, such pleas ultimately failed, for under the terms of that covenant no provision was made to ensure the attaining of that to which they were called. The blessings remained out of reach; hence, the need for a new covenant. Under this new covenant such pleas will be unnecessary, for the knowledge of God will be co-extensive with the covenant community itself. God's people—each of them individually—will know God and enjoy his fellowship. Caught up in this promise is the doctrine of reconciliation both judicially or positionally realized, and experientially realized by means of God's Spirit. Amazingly, this majestic God of eternity, eternally self-sufficient and content in the fellowship of his triune persons, has in grace opened himself to his people, sinful though they are, and brought them into covenantal, loving fellowship with himself. Certainly, in one sense, God was with his old covenant people—this was the great significance of the tabernacle. But the people had access only representatively, by means of the high priest. The knowledge of God was mediated. Thus the writer of Hebrews can say, speaking in broad strokes, that access to God was "not yet" (Heb. 9:8). The old covenant made no such provision. Israel was kept at a distance. The people of God had no right to enter the holiest place. But in the coming day, God says, under this new covenant that he will make with his people, "they will all know me, from the least of them to the greatest. I will be their God, and they will be my people."

3. Forgiveness of Sin

Finally, this covenant provides for full and complete forgiveness of sins. "For I will forgive their iniquity, and I will remember their sin no more" (Jer. 31:34). Ezekiel says the same in terms of old covenant ritual cleansings: "I will sprinkle clean water on you, and you will be clean; I will cleanse you from all your impurities and from all your idols.... I will save you from all your uncleanness" (Ezek. 36:25, 29). In both cases the language is that of justification and, of course, points forward to a substitute by whose sacrifice the penalty of sin is paid in full, thus satisfying the just demands of a righteous God. Covenants were customarily ratified in blood. Often an animal was cut in half—

hence the expression, "cutting a covenant"—and both parties of the covenant passed between the halves as if to say, "So shall it happen to me if ever I violate the terms of this covenant" (cf. Jer. 34:18). Interestingly, in Genesis 15 it is not God and Abraham but God alone who passes between the two halves of the slain animal, as if to hold only himself responsible for the keeping of the covenant. This was a unilateral covenant, a covenant made to depend on God alone, and God himself takes the oath and the responsibility.[7] Abraham merely trusted him to do what he had promised, "and it was counted to him for righteousness." And so it is with this new covenant— ratified not in the blood of any animal but in the blood of Christ. "This cup is the covenant in my blood which is shed for many for the remission of sins" (Matt. 26:28; cf. Mark 14:24; Luke 22:20; 1 Cor. 11:25). He has borne the curse due us and thus secured our forgiveness.

We must be careful to notice the explanatory conjunction—"for" or "because" (_ki_, 31:34). God will give a new heart and enter graciously into covenant fellowship with his people _because_ he will forgive their sins. Sin was the first obstacle, and its removal was necessary to secure other blessings that follow. Here, then, is the ground on which all

---

[7] Some have argued on the ground of the required obedience stated in Genesis 17 and 22 that the Abrahamic covenant is not unilateral / unconditional after all. Alternatively, this has led others to posit two Abrahamic covenants, one conditional and one unconditional. But it is probably easiest to understand these required demands within the larger framework of God's initiative and promise to affect every covenanted blessing, in which case the demanded obedience is not left uncertain.

of God's blessings come to his people. It is only *because of* the substitutionary work of Christ that results in our justification that other covenant blessings are given. This is the only ground. All our standing with God is secured by the objective work of our Surety. Because he has taken our obligations as his own, and because he has stood in our place bearing the curse of our sin, God does not and cannot remember our sins against us any longer. They are gone, cast away as far as the east is from the west. The debt has been paid, and justice demands our acquittal. On this ground every covenant blessing is secured. That is to say, though our regeneration was a work of the Spirit, it was a work secured for us in Christ's blood. Similarly, our progressive sanctification and perseverance are blessings secured for us in the sacrifice of Christ. Our fellowship with God now and forever was purchased once and for all in the cross work of our Redeemer. All we have and are before God comes freely to us, but only because it was purchased for us by the blood of the Lord Jesus. Jesus reflects this understanding when he institutes the Lord's Supper as the sign of the new covenant and speaks of forgiveness as its essential purpose—"This is my blood of the covenant, which is poured out for many for the forgiveness of sins." This covenant is sealed in Christ's blood and has, as the ground for its every provision, pardon for sin secured in the sacrifice of the Redeemer.

The writer of the letter to the Hebrews (chapters 9-10) takes up this matter in reference to the previous blessing promised—fellowship with God. We are not likely to consider well enough the staggering privilege it is to enjoy the presence and fellowship of God. So a great part of the old covenant was designed to teach us just this point. But it accomplished this by reminding us repeatedly that we have no right to the presence and fellowship of God. It did not take long under the old covenant to learn that it is a fearful thing to enter the presence of God. No one is good enough, and no one has that right. If even an animal sets foot on that mountain when God is there, run it through with a spear—it has no right to be so close. And so when God gave the law, the people said to Moses, "You go up! Don't let him speak to us lest we die!" When the Ark of the Covenant was returned to Israel, some of the men of Beth Shemesh just had to look inside. And so God killed them and struck the people with a plague. The lesson was clear, "Who can stand in the presence of the LORD, this holy God?" (1 Sam. 6:20). No man has that right. Uzzah failed to learn from history and put out his hand to steady the ark as it was being transported to Jerusalem. When he touched it, he died. He had no right to come so close. Gentiles, of course, were on the outside altogether and not part of the people of God, and so in the temple there were signs allowing Gentiles to proceed no farther. As a Gentile, you could proselytize to that old covenant community, but still there were barriers. Though an Israelite, you still would not be a priest, and only the Levite priests could go into the holy place. You must worship from afar. Even so, there was a thick veil barring entrance to the holiest place. Even the priests had no right—they too must stay back. Of that priestly clan, only those of the family of Aaron could go beyond that curtain, only the high priest. But even he could dare approach only once a year, and that only after careful preparations were made and prescriptions followed. If he

violated those prescriptions he would be stricken dead. No
man has the right to enter beyond the veil into the presence
of God. It is a fearful thing to approach this God. And the
old covenant shouted this warning—"You, sinner, dare not
presume! Don't get too close. You have no right." Hebrews
9:7-8 tells us that the old system was designed to teach us
just this point.

But a strange thing happened when Christ died. That
veil in the temple was torn from top to bottom—from top
to bottom, not from bottom to top, presumably signifying
that this was a work of God. And what could this mean but
that the way to God was now open? That by the death of
Jesus Christ there is new access to God! And so the writer
to the Hebrews, after citing this new covenant prophecy
from Jeremiah, says,

> *Therefore, brothers, since we have confidence to enter the*
> *Most Holy Place by the blood of Jesus, by a new and living way*
> *opened for us through the curtain, that is, his body, and since*
> *we have a great priest over the house of God, let us draw near*
> *to God with a sincere heart in full assurance of faith, having*
> *our hearts sprinkled to cleanse us from a guilty conscience and*
> *having our bodies washed with pure water* (Heb. 10:19-22).

Here is that wonderful New Testament—new covenant!—word, *access*. By the blood of Christ we are given
access, brought into the very presence of God, to know him
and to enjoy fellowship with him, and so we are invited,
amazingly, not only to draw near but to draw near with
boldness. This access to God could be accomplished in no
other way—it is given to us *because* in Christ we have been
forgiven, and that which barred us from fellowship with
God is remembered against us no more. A new record and
a new standing have been given us, and we now have

access. What an awesome privilege this is. This is the new covenant.

The Fulfillment of this Covenant

In all this we have already begun to answer the question of when this covenant is fulfilled. Hebrews 8 and 10 specifically relate it to the present experience of the Christian who may rejoice in the knowledge of sins forgiven. By means of the blood of Christ, our sins are all gone, never to be remembered against us. 2 Corinthians 3 likewise speaks not only of our justification, but also of our regeneration and sanctification by the Spirit of God powerfully at work in us, transforming us into the image of Christ from glory to glory. These new covenant provisions are precisely what we celebrate each time we come to the Lord's Table, and by its symbols are reminded of what Christ has accomplished for us. The age of the new covenant has dawned. Our sins are forgiven. The Spirit has come, and we are a radically _changed_ people. The language of the prophecy goes beyond the returned exiles from Babylon and reaches to us in the church, to all who are in Christ.

Yet in Romans 11:26-27 the apostle Paul specifically relates the new covenant promise of forgiveness to a point in the future—when "the Deliverer will come from Zion." And so this covenant has evidently not yet reached its climactic fulfillment.

In fact, we ourselves wonder at times if the blessings we have received, wonderful as they are, are really what is held out for us in this covenant. To be sure, we enjoy these blessings in our experience today. But, then again, we do not. God has given us a new heart, and we feel it. From our hearts we want now to follow God faithfully. We love him, and we want deeply to obey him and live for him. The Spirit is ours, and there has been real life-transformation — we are not what we used to be! But even so, very frankly, we sometimes feel like we have *two* hearts, one that moves us to follow God and another that pulls us away. We serve God, but so often we wonder if we have ever served him with a pure heart and a pure motive. We set our minds on things above (and we are most joyful when we do), but it is a constant and difficult struggle to do so. We also set our minds on things below, even sinful things, and we do not always or even terribly consistently walk according to God's law as this covenant promises. The fact is, our heart is inclined to obey, and our heart is inclined *not* to obey. There is a kind of schizophrenia about us — the flesh still wars against the Spirit and the Spirit against the flesh. We feel that we live in two worlds — redeemed out of this present evil world yet remaining in it, and all too often conforming to it. Not at all to minimize the greatness of his work in us, it often seems but half done. God has begun a good work in us, and it is very evident that he has. But it is just as evident that this work is not yet complete. For whatever obedience we have rendered, still every day we find ourselves before God in that humiliating exercise of confession of sin. The great new covenant promises are now, but surely they are also not yet.

So while we rejoice in the great privilege that is ours today, we long for a better day. The preachers of the new covenant, in both the Old and New Testaments, declare that a day is coming when these great promises will be realized in full, and all this conflict will be behind us. In that day there will be no need for laws to be posted — "You shall have no other gods before me!" "You shall not kill!" "You shall not hate or mistreat your neighbor!" "You shall not commit adultery!" "You shall not lust!" "Do not yield your members to sin!" Or even, "Set your affections on things above!" God's work in us will be so thoroughly perfected that all such laws will then be superfluous. In that day, we will love God with all our heart and soul and mind and strength, and we will love our neighbor as we love ourselves. The long-anticipated "glory" of moral transformation promised in the new covenant will then be finally realized in full. Today we have the firstfruits of the Spirit, the first installment of the new covenant promise. But in that day we will not have the firstfruits but the final and full harvest of his powerful, transforming presence. And with all of our hearts and for all eternity and without exception in time or in degree our hearts will be his, and his work in us will be complete. Changed from glory to glory throughout this day, in that day we will take our place _in_ glory, then made like our Savior. O, what that day will be like! The heart throb of God's people throughout this inaugurated new covenant age has been—"Come, Lord Jesus, come! Take away our bent to sinning! Finish the new creation! Come, Lord Jesus, come!" This is our great hope. We may be assured, for God has sworn by himself (for he could swear by no greater) in covenant oath, that the day will come and bring this hope of glory to realization.

In that day our access to God will be perfect, for we shall live in his very presence—"We shall see his face!" "We shall see him as he is." In that day, we are told, there will be no need of the sun, for God and the Lamb will be there.

There will be no temple, for God and the Lamb will be there. We are told there will be no more sickness and no more crying and no more death and no more of the struggles that mark this life. And all this because there will be no more sin and no more curse—our sins will have been cast away as far as east is from west. Forever we will bask in the glory of the presence of our gracious covenant-making and covenant-keeping God. How our hearts throb to hear the great announcement, "Now the dwelling of God is with men, and he will live with them. They will be his people, and God himself will be with them and be their God."

> Then we shall be where we would be!
> Then we shall be what we should be!
> Things that are not now nor could be
> Soon shall be our own!

So we enjoy today the first installment of these great covenant blessings. What wonderful blessings they are! Our great redeemer appeared once at the end of the ages to secure these blessings for us by the sacrifice of himself, but we wait with hearts desperate to see him come a second time to bring this great salvation to its glorious culmination. Then, finally in his blessed presence, these promises will all be realized in fullest measure. Then we will be his people and only his. Then we will know him, for we will be with him. Then our hearts will be his truly—his only, and his forever.

Until then, from the bottom of our hearts we sing with all the church, "Oh! Lord Jesus, how long?" And with hearts full of eager anticipation we pray, "Come! Lord Jesus, come quickly!"

Implications for New Covenant Theology

We have surveyed in broad strokes the nature and provisions of the new covenant, and now we take the next and more delicate step and seek to outline some of its hermeneutical consequences. Specifically, what are the essentials and leading marks of a theology that is rightly oriented to the new covenant?

A Pronounced Christocentricity

We have seen that the new covenant drives our attention to the Lord Jesus Christ who, by his death, secures all its promised blessings. Taking up in itself as it does the expectations of the Abrahamic and Davidic covenants (Ezek. 16:60-63; 34:23-31), the drive is only more compelling. God's redemptive purpose promised throughout the centuries climaxes in Christ.

To anyone who has been a Christian for any length of time, it is a simple truism that the Bible is a book about Christ. The New Testament is so stamped by the idea of fulfillment that it just cannot be missed. All that was anticipated in the Old Testament is realized in the New in the person of the Lord Jesus Christ. He is the champion of the woman's seed, the seed of Abraham, the ideal nation, the new Moses, the better priest, the Lamb of God, the new temple, the Sabbath, the manna from heaven, the greater Joshua, the faithful servant, the faithful son, David's great-er son, the stone of offense—these prophecies, types, and expectations and so many more are all brought to their intended fulfillment in the person and work of our Lord. Even a first reading of the New Testament cannot mistake the idea of fulfillment thrown in such strong relief by John the Baptist, the New Testament writers, and our Lord him-self. "Moses wrote of me" (John 5:46) is our Lord's claim, and as the New Testament unfolds his claim becomes ever more evident.

To say this much is to say also that it is not just the New Testament but also the Old Testament that is written about Jesus. Again, this is Jesus' claim exactly.

Matthew 5:17

> *Do not think that I have come to abolish the Law or the Prophets; I have not come to abolish them but to fulfill them.*

Luke 10:23-24

> *Then he turned to his disciples and said privately, "Blessed are the eyes that see what you see. For I tell you that many prophets and kings wanted to see what you see but did not see it, and to hear what you hear but did not hear it."*

Luke 24:27

> *And beginning with Moses and all the Prophets, he ex-plained to them what was said in all the Scriptures concerning himself.*

Luke 24:44

> *He said to them, "This is what I told you while I was still with you: Everything must be fulfilled that is written about me in the Law of Moses, the Prophets and the Psalms."*

John 5:39, 46

> These are the Scriptures that testify about me... If you be-
> lieved Moses, you would believe me, for he wrote about me.

John 8:56

> Your father Abraham rejoiced at the thought of seeing my
> day; he saw it and was glad.

Hebrews 10:7

> Then I said, "Here I am—it is written about me in the
> scroll—I have come to do your will, O God."

Both from the perspective of BC and AD and in terms of
expectation and hope and of realization and fulfillment, the
Bible in its entirety is a book about Jesus Christ.

Moreover, although fulfillment is the dominant note of
the New Testament, the note of hope remains. The new
covenant age has dawned, but its fullness awaits the day of
Christ. Caught between these two ages, we both rejoice in
the realization of the promised blessings and cry with hope
for their full and final realization.

Something of all this expectation, fulfillment, and yet
remaining expectation is built into Scripture's revelation of
law in the old and new covenants, respectively. Jesus' claim
to "fulfill" the law of Moses (Matt. 5:17) leads us to this
understanding exactly. "Fulfill" (*pleroō*) in Matthew consistently carries the idea of bringing to realization what
was previously anticipated. Implicit in his claim to fulfill
the law is the assertion that the old covenant law pointed
forward to him in some way. This is what Jesus states explicitly in Matthew 11:13—"For all the Prophets and the
Law prophesied until John." And so in his exposition of his
"fulfillment" of Moses' law—"You have heard it said...but
I say to you" (Matt. 5:21ff)—Jesus describes the law of his
kingdom as that of which Moses' law was but an anticipa-

tion. Hence, "You shall not murder" becomes absorbed in a prohibition of unwarranted anger and mistreatment of others; "You shall not commit adultery" becomes absorbed in a prohibition of lust; the regulated provision for divorce is lost in a prohibition of divorce; the insistence on keeping one's oath issues into a demand for general truth-telling ; the *lex talionis* is replaced with a call for non-resistance; and "love your neighbor and hate your enemy" becomes instead "love your enemy." What is Jesus up to in all this? What is the hermeneutical consideration driving him? He tells us: his law "fulfills" the old. It brings about what the old law could only anticipate. As we have seen, in the consummated kingdom precisely all of these laws will have been rendered superfluous—there, with our transformation complete, we scarcely will need to be told "Do not kill." But this in-between age itself brings about an advance on Moses that moves us in that eschatological direction. Here, in the inaugurated kingdom, "Do not hate" and "Do not lust" so far outstrip "Do not murder" and "Do not commit adultery" that the older laws could seem superfluous. Something of the coming age has been pulled backward into this age, and in this community of Christ there is both a fulfillment of what was anticipated in the Mosaic community and a glimpse and anticipation of what the coming age will be when it is realized in full.

Once again, all this to say that the law of Christ constitutes an advance on Moses. This is not to say Moses is useless, but it is to say that he has taken a back seat to Christ, the new Moses, the new lawgiver, who has "fulfilled" what Moses' law could only anticipate. This, simply, is Jesus' claim in Matthew 5:17-48.

Note that all this must inform our answer to the question raised earlier regarding the identity of "my law" in Jeremiah 31:33. Just what is the content of "God's law" that is inscribed on the heart of the new covenant believer? Here in Matthew 5:17ff our Lord informs us that whatever Mosaic law we wish to say remains in force must be understood only as filtered through him, its fulfillment. "The continuing practice of the commandments of the law must be viewed in light of their fulfillment by Jesus. It is the law *as fulfilled by Jesus* that must be done, not the law in its original form."[8] Ultimately, Jeremiah 31:33 points to God's law in its new covenant form.

We will touch on more of this as we go along, but for now it is enough simply to demonstrate that this is how our Lord has taught us to read our Bibles. From beginning to end, from expectation to fulfillment to further expectation, its many strands all converge in him. In this way new covenant theology seeks to follow the Bible's metanarrative—a metanarrative that has as its culminating theme, in more ways than can be counted, the Lord Jesus Christ. And within this larger context we look expectantly to find new aspects of our Lord's glory. This Christocentric redemptive-historical hermeneutic is of course not unique to us, but it is by all counts a primary undergirding factor for what we have today come to call new covenant theology. Themes such as covenant, law, and new covenant are interpreted and understood on this grid.

---

[8] Moo, "The Law of Christ as the Fulfillment of the Law of Moses," p. 358 (emphasis his).

The Priority of New Covenant Revelation

The Advance of the New over the Old

To say this much leaves implications, one of which is the implicit and often explicit recognition of the priority of new covenant revelation. The advance of the new covenant Scriptures over the old covenant Scriptures is massive. The former anticipates Christ; the latter proclaims his arrival. The former is marked by hope; the latter is marked by fulfillment. Throughout all the previous centuries God spoke to the fathers and the prophets in various ways at various times, but now his revelation has reached its zenith in the coming of his own Son who, in his own life and teachings, and by his Spirit through his apostles, has spoken with climactic finality (Heb. 1:1-2). In short, the revelation of this new covenant so far surpasses that of the old that the old pales by comparison.

This theme of the advance of the new revelation over the old is stressed in a web of various emphases in the teaching of Jesus and the New Testament writers. Basically, it is understood simply in that the new covenant itself surpasses and replaces the old—a theme we will unpack further in due course. But this theme is presented in many other ways also. Prophecies, types, and anticipations of every kind in the Old Testament move us forward to Christ who is greater than Moses, greater than all the prophets, greater than David, greater than the temple, greater than the Sabbath, and so on. They all point us to the one of whom God said, "This is my beloved Son, hear him!"

This is precisely the announcement of John's prologue (John 1:1-18). Christ is God's incarnate Word, God speaking if you will. In Jesus not only are centuries of silence broken, but all the prophets are eclipsed as in his life and words the invisible God makes himself known.

The claim our Lord Jesus made, and the claim the New Testament writers make of him, is that he is God's supreme self-disclosure. His teaching marks the highest point of divine revelation. But it should be noted that the revelation of God that came by his Son is not restricted to Christ's words only—the red letters in your New Testament. The fullness of his revelation comes to us by means of his apostles. This is what Jesus himself promised in his discussion of his provision of the Holy Spirit in John 14-16. He himself was leaving, but he would send his Spirit to his apostles to continue his teaching to them, so that they, in turn, would bring his teaching to the church.

> He who does not love Me does not keep My words; and the word which you hear is not Mine but the Father's who sent Me. These things I have spoken to you while being present with you. But the Helper, the Holy Spirit, whom the Father will send in My name, He will teach you all things, and bring to your remembrance all things that I said to you (John 14:24-26).

> I still have many things to say to you, but you cannot bear them now. However, when He, the Spirit of truth, has come, He will guide you into all truth; for He will not speak on His own authority, but whatever He hears He will speak; and He will tell you things to come. He will glorify Me, for He will take of what is Mine and declare it to you. All things that the Father has are Mine. Therefore I said that He will take of Mine and declare it to you (John 16:12-15).

> For I gave them the words you gave me and they accepted them. They knew with certainty that I came from you, and they believed that you sent me...As you sent me into the world, I

*have sent them into the world ...My prayer is not for them
alone. I pray also for those who will believe in me through their
message* (John 17:8, 18, 20; cf. 1 John 1:1-3).

Our Lord has provided for the preservation of his teaching in the ministry of his apostles. Here in the new covenant Scriptures, God's revelation has reached its highest
point to date.

A New Orientation

Once again, all of this carries implications. If our attention is being drawn climactically to Christ, then what of
Moses? And if we are given a new covenant, then what is
the status of the old? What is the nature of this eclipse of
the new over the old? And in what way does this shape the
orientation of the new covenant believer?

In 2 Corinthians 3 the apostle emphasizes that his is not
a ministry of the old covenant but of the new (vv. 1-3, 6),
and he speaks of the old covenant in the past tense as one
whose day is past (v. 7), having been surpassed by the
superior glory of the new (vv. 7-11). He argues along these
lines in Galatians 3:19-25, that the historical purpose of the
law was temporal—it was given to serve as Israel's guardi-
an until Christ came. That is to say, the law had a historical
beginning (Moses) and a historical end (Christ). A similar
point is made in Hebrews 8 where the writer plainly expresses a replacement theology in which the old covenant
has given way to the new—"By calling this covenant 'new'
he has made the first one obsolete" (v. 13; cf. v. 7). Similarly, in Hebrews 7:11-12 the writer reasons simply that the
new (i.e., Melchizedekan) priesthood stands as declaration
and proof positive that there has been a change of law. The
law was grounded in the Levitical priesthood; thus, the

inspired writer reasons, by the nature of the case there must have been a change of law also. Shadow has given way to substance, and there is a resulting redemptive-historical shift from the old to the new.

So we are not surprised to hear the apostle Paul exhort believers to stand fast in their freedom from the old law and refuse to submit to it (Gal. 5:1). Nor are we surprised to hear him refer to requirements of the old law as "nothing"—"Circumcision is nothing, and uncircumcision is nothing. Keeping God's commands is what counts" (1 Cor. 7:19). Such a statement would horrify an old covenant believer—how dare you call circumcision "nothing"? And where do you get off *contrasting* circumcision with the commands of God? Circumcision *is* a command of God! But no, Paul says, the new covenant believer has a new orientation. The commands of God to which he is obliged are not defined for him by the older revelation but by the new revelation in Christ. And in this new revelation, God's former command of circumcision is nothing.

Again, in 1 Corinthians 9:20-21 the apostle reflects the same reorientation:

> *To the Jews I became like a Jew, to win the Jews. To those under the law I became like one under the law (though I myself am not under the law), so as to win those under the law. To those not having the law I became like one not having the law (though I am not free from God's law but am under Christ's law), so as to win those not having the law.*

Note that Paul does not consider himself as first obliged to the old law (of Moses) but able to exercise some liberty when necessary. He expressly says that he is "not under the law." But neither is he without obligations altogether, for he is "under the law of Christ." This, he says, is his orientation—it is not Mosaic but Christocentric. As a new covenant believer he very naturally looks to the stipulations of the new covenant as his rule of life. This "third" position for the apostle—neither obligated to Moses nor without law altogether but under Christ's law—would be appalling to one whose orientation is to the old covenant. But Paul has learned that Moses has been eclipsed, and it is to the revelation in Christ that he looks.

It is of further interest here to note the contrasting expressions, "not under the law" and "under Christ's law." Paul describes the Jews as "under law"—that is, under the law of Moses. This is his regular expression *hupo nomon*. But he does not use this expression to describe his new status as a Christian. He does not say that he is *hupo nomon Christou* (under the law of Christ). Rather, he says that he is *ennomos Christou*. This phrase is notoriously difficult to translate, but "in-lawed to Christ" is a common rendering. Whatever exact translation uncertainties there may be, what is significant is that Paul does not see these two contrasting positions as exactly parallel. The Jews were "under law." But Paul the Christian is, very literally, "in-lawed to Christ." For Paul the believer there has not been only a switching over of laws, with a new orientation to Christ, there is a differing status also. He is no longer "under law" but "in Christ," and he understands his ethical orientation accordingly.[9]

---

[9] Hence BAGD suggests the translation, "under the jurisdiction of Christ."

The Status of the Decalogue

This, in turn, raises the more specific (and more delicate) question of the status of the Decalogue in this new covenant age. It is common among Reformed interpreters to insist that the Decalogue is unchangeable and eternally binding, but this seems difficult to square with the exegetical data. In its first instance, the Decalogue is the foundational statement of the old covenant. It would seem impossible to speak of the "obsolescence" (Heb. 8:13) of the old covenant while leaving the Decalogue untouched. In fact Paul specifies that it is not just the old covenant, generally, that has passed away but the Decalogue itself, the law "written on stone" (2 Cor. 3:7-11).

This does not imply that such things as graven images and taking the Lord's name in vain are no longer forbidden, to be sure! But it at least means that the Decalogue as such has been surpassed. It no longer stands as the believer's point of reference. We have just observed this from the apostle Paul in 1 Corinthians 7:19 and 9:20-21. "Since we are in-lawed" to Christ, our reference point has shifted accordingly. This, in turn, seems clearly to preclude the understanding of the Decalogue as an eternal and unchanging standard. An objective standard remains, but with Paul our orientation has shifted from Moses to Christ, and it is in the law of Christ—indeed, in Christ!—we find our rule of life. So while we continue in this age to reference the Decalogue in shaping our behavior, we no longer reference it on its own terms: we reference the Decalogue—indeed, as we reference the entire Old Testament—in light of its fulfillment in Christ.

The Sabbath in the New Covenant

Of course, the point of most notable dispute in this regard is the question of the Sabbath and how it is to be observed today. If we begin with the presupposition that the
Decalogue is the eternal, unchanging moral law of God,
then the discussion is over and the traditional Reformed
interpretation stands. But as we have just seen, this presupposition deserves to be challenged on exegetical
grounds. More to our point here, the New Testament writers consistently treat the Sabbath as having served an anticipatory function, a purpose and usefulness exhausted in
the person and work of Christ. Under the new covenant all
of life has been made holy, and as a result there are no
special holy days (Rom. 14; Gal. 4:9-11; Col. 2:16-17). In
particular, the Sabbath day pictured a rest now realized in
Christ (Matt. 11:28-30; Col. 2:16-17; Heb. 4), and according
to Galatians 4:9-11 a return to Sabbath-keeping is wholly
inconsistent with the Christian profession. In short, reading
our Bibles Christocentrically and recognizing the priority of
new covenant revelation we are made to see that the Sabbath had an anticipatory function which, once realized,
rendered it obsolete.

Just as it should not surprise us to find extensive continuity between the old and new covenants, so it should not
surprise us to find areas of discontinuity as well. The foundational statement of the old covenant should not be as-
sumed to be the binding law of the new covenant. It is left
to the covenant giver to determine such things. Nor should
we expect the sign of the old covenant, which in its first
instance was the function of the Sabbath (Exod. 31), to be
carried over into the new. Reading our Bibles as we do we
are not surprised to find that the Sabbath is no longer a day

to be observed but a rest enjoyed every day (Rom. 14:5) in Christ. The Sabbath is not thereby destroyed; it is fulfilled (Matt. 5:17).

Our point here is simply that the new covenant believer is oriented to the stipulations of the new covenant, and this is precisely what the New Testament writers reflect in their own teaching and behavior. The new and greater than Moses has come—we are _his_ servants, and it is to his law we look for our rule of life (1 Cor. 9:20-21). So in this new covenant age we "keep the Sabbath" not in the observance of a day of the week as holy but in our faith-rest in Christ. This is the shape of Sabbath-keeping in the new covenant. And thus, we observe the Sabbath today in the way we observe all the old covenant law—in light of Christ, its fulfillment.

The Contrasting Nature of Old and New Covenants

Turning to more fundamental issues, new covenant theology stresses the discontinuity between the old and new covenants. Admittedly, some areas of continuity between these covenants are evident. In Jeremiah 31 the same God who entered into a covenant relationship with Israel at Sinai now announces a new covenant with them, promising many of the same blessings. Through both covenants God's single redemptive purpose is advanced, and both covenants carry the command to keep God's law. But interpreters from the Reformed side have generally seen more continuity than we are willing to acknowledge. Indeed, some have made much over the fact that both the

Hebrew *hadash* and the Greek *kainos* can mean "renewed" or "restored." Thus, it has been argued, the new covenant is not a brand new covenant after all but a renewal of the old, only with the promise that it would be finally breached.

Of the much that could be said in response to this, most telling is the language of the prophecy itself—this new covenant that is yet to be "created" (*bara*, Jer. 31:22) is "not like" the old (31:32), and results in an arrangement in which previous experiences are "no longer" (31:29, 34). This new covenant replaces the old precisely because the old had failed, and the new covenant is therefore radically different from the old. It is this note of discontinuity that Jeremiah emphasizes. In the New Testament it is explicitly stated that the old or "first" has faded away and become obsolete, giving way to the new or "second" (2 Cor. 3:1-6; Heb. 8:7, 13). It could certainly be argued that the hopes and promises entailed in the old covenant are renewed in the new, but it would seem that any significance attached to the notion of "renewal" in this connection must be understood not in reference to the Sinaitic covenant, but to the Abrahamic and Davidic covenants, which, as we have already noted, are taken up and brought to realization in the new covenant. But again, Galatians 3 and Hebrews 8 as well as Jeremiah 31 speak explicitly in terms of this new covenant *replacing* the covenant made at Sinai. This is not a renewal of the Mosaic; it is in fact a *new* covenant given to replace the old.[10] Let us now note the points of contrast.

---

[10] Hence the standard Hebrew and Greek lexicons regularly prefer to define the words *hadash* (Jer. 31:31), *kainos* (Heb. 8:8), and *neos* (Heb.

Difference in Kind

Basic to this discussion is the differing character of the two covenants. The Mosaic covenant was not a grant treaty, like the Abrahamic or the new covenant, in which God makes certain promises and takes all responsibility for the covenant himself. It was a covenant conditioned on obedience and marked by the familiar tone, "If you obey, I will bless; if you do not obey, you will endure covenant curses." This relationship was established at the beginning, when God said to Moses,

> *"Now if you obey me fully and keep my covenant, then out of all nations you will be my treasured possession. Although the whole earth is mine, you will be for me a kingdom of priests and a holy nation. These are the words you are to speak to the Israelites." So Moses went back and summoned the elders of the people and set before them all the words the LORD had commanded him to speak. The people all responded together, "We will do everything the LORD has said"* (Exod. 19:5-8).

This "If you, then I" relationship is repeated throughout the Pentateuch. Leviticus 18:5—"Keep my decrees and laws, for the man who obeys them will live by them. I am the LORD." Deuteronomy 27:26—"Cursed is the man who does not uphold the words of this law by carrying them out." Leviticus 26 is a prominent example, as is Deuteronomy 11:26–32, where Moses sets before the people "a blessing and a curse: the blessing, if you obey the commandments of the Lord your God...and the curse, if you do not obey." Another prominent example is found in Moses'

12:24) in terms of recent existence. See BAGD, Kittel, BDB, TWOT, Koehler & Baumgartner, etc.

farewell discourse, where he presents the nation with the options of "life and good, death and evil" (Deut. 30:15–20). This note is familiar to anyone reading the law and scarcely needs further demonstration here.

But this "if you, then I" is precisely the note missing in the new covenant. In the making of this covenant there is no mutual agreement as there was at Sinai, no "if" clauses at all, and nothing approaching the language of these verses cited above. In fact this covenant is couched in just these terms of contrast. God says this new covenant is not like the old, the one that they broke, and he promises that *this* covenant they will not break. They will not break it simply because it will depend on him alone, and what he requires of them he will bring about in them and for them.

In simple terms, the old covenant was a works covenant; the new covenant is a grace covenant. The apostle Paul characterized the old covenant as one of works: "The law is not based on faith; on the contrary, 'the man who does these things will live by them'" (Gal. 3:12; cf. Lev. 18:5). The old covenant was conditioned on Israel's obedience; the new is unconditional and promissory. The old depended upon the people and what they would do; the new is a covenant God makes not simply with but "to" or "for" (*le*) his people (Hos. 2:18), and depends upon him alone and what he does for its carrying out. The difference between these covenants is the difference between works and grace. The new is an explicitly *gracious* covenant.

Paul takes up this point in Galatians 3 and explores the question of why the law needed to be added if the promise had already been made in the Abrahamic covenant. Clearly, this question would not need to be raised if Paul had understood the old covenant to be gracious in character. The question is raised precisely because the law, works-oriented as it is, may appear to be contrary to the Abrahamic promise previously given. We may be sure that while God had a gracious *purpose* in giving the law, viewed redemptive-historically, the *terms* of that covenant itself were specifically performance-oriented and its blessings conditioned on Israel's obedience.

Renewal and Transformation

This is precisely where the new covenant demonstrates its superiority over the old: what the old covenant could only command the new covenant delivers. The "fault" (Heb. 8:7-8) of the old covenant lay in Israel's inability to bring about the righteousness it required. All the old law written on stone could do is command—make obligation plain—and then condemn all failure. The law was a hard taskmaster indeed. It would command and then leave it to you to find the will and strength to obey, throw you back on the strength of your own arm, and demand compliance under pain of death.

> Run, run and work the law demands,
> But gives me neither feet nor hands.

It was, in Paul's words, a law of "letter" only. It could not reach the inner man and bring about transformation and willing obedience. As a law of external letters only all it could do was command and condemn. Its thunderous demands could strike fear, but they could affect no change. In Paul's words again, it was a law that could only "minister death."

By contrast, this new and gracious covenant promises better things. Whatever obligations are implied on the human side by the "law written on the heart," Jeremiah makes it clear that it will not ultimately depend on the people to fulfill these obligations. God has taken this on himself. This is a work he will do in his people. Moses complained that the people had no heart to comply with the law's demands (Deut. 5:29). But the demands of this new covenant are not merely engraved on stone or written in letters with ink but etched on the human heart. The naturally hard, unimpressionable heart is replaced with a heart of flesh. Indeed God's Spirit himself comes in renewing and morally transforming power to bring about in us exactly what He demands of us.

> Run, run and work the law demands,
> But gives me neither feet nor hands.
> But sweeter news the gospel brings –
> It bids me fly and lends me wings!

This is the ground of the often-repeated New Testament emphasis on what Warfield called "the great change"—the radical transformation of the human heart and life in regeneration, conversion, and growth in godliness. "It is God who works in us both to will and do of his good pleasure" (Phil. 2:13). The virtues incumbent on and evident in the Christian are the Spirit's fruit supernaturally produced in us.

> *What the law was powerless to do in that it was weakened by the sinful nature, God did by sending his own Son in the likeness of sinful man to be a sin offering. And so he condemned sin in sinful man, in order that the righteous requirements of the law might be fully met in us, who do not live according to the sinful nature but according to the Spirit* (Rom. 8:3-4).

Simply put, in this new covenant, what God requires he provides. This is the essence of Augustine's famous prayer that upset Pelagius so—"Lord, give what you command, and command what you will." This is new covenant talk. This is the age of the Spirit. The "life" this covenant ministers (2 Cor. 3:6) is not merely judicial but vital and experiential as well.

Forgiveness, Justification, and Fellowship with God

Moreover, the old covenant made no provisions for law-breakers—only condemnation. If ever and wherever you failed, the law could only condemn. It made no provision for transgression. It was a ministry of death. "Do and live; fail and die" is all it had to say. Even its sacrifices offered no final answer. They were only provisional at best. All the old covenant could do was demonstrate sin and the need of grace and thereby throw you back on the promise of grace to Abraham. Taking up that Abrahamic promise, in the new covenant God takes responsibility for sin himself. "So shall it happen to me if I do not keep the terms of this covenant." And so to enact this new covenant *he* is slain. *He* suffers the consequences of sin. *He* bears the curse and wrath of his own justice as *he* stands in the place of sinners, and becomes their surety and substitute.

> Bearing shame and scoffing rude,
> In *my* place condemned *he* stood;
> Sealed *my* pardon with *his* blood –
> Hallelujah! What a Savior!
>
> I hear the accuser roar
> Of ills that I have done
> I know them well and thousands more
> Jehovah findeth none.

Though the restless foe accuses,
Sins recounting like a flood
Every charge our God refuses
Christ has answered with his blood.

Entering that old covenant the people pledged, "All that the Lord has spoken, we will do." Entering this new covenant we confess that we have done nothing but transgress and that our Redeemer has done for us all that God has required of us.

Mine is the sin, but thine the righteousness;
Mine is the guilt, but thine the cleansing blood.

This, the writer to the Hebrews says so aptly, is not only a new and a different covenant but a *better* covenant resting on better promises and boasting a better priest. This covenant, so unlike the old, the apostle Paul says, is not a ministration of death but of life. Graciously, yet in full keeping with justice, this covenant provides cleansing and justification for sinners. The righteousness it demands it freely gives. It brings guilty rebels into the very presence of God, beyond the veil, and there, sinful though they are, they approach the throne, not timidly and with fear, but boldly and with the free and open access of children coming to a loving father.

The writer to the Hebrews stresses the point that under the old covenant there were sacrifices, but those sacrifices were merely a reminder of sin (Heb.10:3). Year after year the sacrifices were offered, continuously for centuries on end. His point is that to any thinking Israelite, this sacrifice which spoke of atonement was but a reminder of sin. Why else would it need to be repeated, but that sin remained and the previous year's sacrifice did not bring about the forgiveness of which it spoke? If atonement were indeed accomplished, then why should it need to be offered again and again and again? Its very repetition was a declaration that sin had not, in fact, been put away, and so it was offered again and again. Thus, each year the offerer was reminded afresh that he had sinned and still stood in need of forgiveness. In the very sacrifice he offered he was reminded of sin.

By contrast, under this new covenant and observing its rite, the Lord's Table, we have a reminder not of sin, but of Christ, in whose blood the promised forgiveness was accomplished once for all. The difference is one of "do" versus "done." Under the old there was the regular reminder of sin; under the new there is a regular reminder of forgiveness. A better covenant indeed!

So Paul argues in 2 Corinthians 3 that the righteousness God demands is in the new covenant provided. Both in terms of judicial standing and of experienced renewal and transformation, this covenant delivers what the old could only require. It provides both willing compliance with God's law and pardon for transgressors of that law. The glory of the old covenant has faded and given way to the surpassing glory of the new. The old was a ministry of death and condemnation; the new is a ministry of life and righteousness. In this way the old covenant pointed away from itself to the new covenant gospel of grace in Christ Jesus.

Eternally Sure and Indestructible

All this serves to emphasize yet another quality of the new covenant. Precisely because this covenant provides all it demands, it is an eternal and indestructible covenant.

Jeremiah, Ezekiel, Isaiah, and Hosea all refer to this covenant as an "eternal" or "everlasting" covenant (*berith olam;*
Jer. 32-33 [cf. 32:40]; 50:5; Ezek. 16:60; 37:26; Isa. 24:5; 55:3;
61:8; cf. Hos. 2:14-23), a covenant that will never be re-
voked. It will stand as long as creation itself and even longer (Jer. 31:35-36). It is irrevocable simply because God has
taken it on himself to bring about all that is necessary for its
continuation and preservation. He provides forgiveness for
law-breakers, he instills a heart to obey, and he provides
free access to himself for his people in intimate fellowship
with him. The blessings of this covenant are promised to be
brought about in full measure to all his covenant people.
Unlike the old covenant that this replaces, the new covenant will never fail. We have God's word on it—the stars
would fall first.

Aside: The Role of the Law in Sanctification

Once again all this carries implications, and one that is
of interest to this discussion is the role of law in sanctification. Under the new covenant the law, having exhausted its
curse upon our Substitute, has lost its condemning power.
It never did have power to effect the virtue it demanded,
and it no longer carries even the terror it formerly held
over us. God's law has been written on our hearts, and
obedience now stems from the supernatural workings of
the Spirit of God within us. The law still informs our con-
science, but it no longer rules in it with its former threaten-
ings. Both our initial renewal and our continued transformation are a work undertaken for us and in us by God's
Spirit.

Paul argues this in vivid terms in 2 Corinthians 3. The
great transformation evident in the lives of the believers

there stands as vindicating proof of Paul's new covenant ministry in which the Holy Spirit removes blindness and gives a new sight of Christ that continues throughout life to shape us into the image of Christ, as from glory to glory. In Galatians the argument is the same. It is no longer the law that marks out God's people—that way failed. It is the Spirit, producing his fruit in us, who powerfully marks us out as belonging to God.

It is interesting what Paul says is the precise means the Spirit uses in this ongoing process of moral transformation. "And we, who with unveiled faces all reflect the Lord's glory, are being transformed into his likeness with ever-increasing glory" (2 Cor. 3:18). He does not say that the Spirit rivets our attention to God's law so as to cause us to obey. Rather, he increasingly acquaints us with the Scripture's glorious portrayal of Christ, and by that acquaintance with his glory we ourselves are transformed into his likeness from glory to glory. That is to say, there is in the gospel itself the "stuff" which the Holy Spirit uses to transform us.

Sailhamer suggests a possible hint of this in the Pentateuch itself. The point is made in Genesis 26:5 that Abraham was obedient to God's laws. By contrast, Moses, because of his unfaithfulness and disobedience, was not allowed to enter the promised land. The implication just may be—already, way back in the Pentateuch itself—that only promise (Abraham) and not the law (Moses) can effect genuine obedience.[11]

---

[11] John H. Sailhamer, _Introduction to Old Testament Theology_ (Grand Rapids: Zondervan Publishing House, 1995), pp. 260-71.

This thinking is reflected in Ephesians 3:13-19 where the apostle expresses his conviction that an increased acquaintance with the love of Christ will result in our spiritual strengthening. Similarly in Titus 3:4-8 he insists that by the faithful teaching of the freeness of salvation in Christ believers are given incentive to maintain good works.

This same apostle is very willing to cite God's law whenever and wherever needed. God's commands are never irrelevant. He is not without law, and law for him is objective and canonical. But in his desire to see believers further transformed into the likeness of Christ his orientation is to Christ himself and not the law. He does not now assume that the law suddenly has an ability to transform. Rather, he assumes that the Spirit of God continuously transforms the inner man by means of an increasing acquaintance with the new covenant gospel of grace in Christ. In this way, he progressively brings about in us the compliance to God's law that he promised. There is a Christocentricity to the new covenant that extends even to the experience of progressive sanctification.

The Newness of the New Covenant Community

Finally, all this brings us to another fundamental distinctive of new covenant theology, and perhaps the most radical difference between the old and new covenants themselves—the newness of the new covenant community.

On one level, the newness of this new covenant community is seen in that it is inclusive of Gentiles. This would have been something of a surprising thing to Israel—and in fact it *was* surprising even to the believing Jewish Christians of the first century. In Acts we read of their struggles with this very question. But that Gentiles should be brought to share in Israel's covenanted blessings should not have been entirely surprising even from the perspective of the Old Testament. As far back as Abraham we are told that God intends by him to bring blessing to all the families of the earth (Gen. 12:1-3). Jeremiah introduces his message and ministry with the declaration that from his mother's womb he was appointed as a prophet to the nations (Jer. 1:5). It would seem that this prophetic ministry to the nations would include its promissory as well as its condemnatory aspects. In fact, Jeremiah 12:14-17 offers a clear example, where Israel's neighbors are offered the same hopes of Israel upon the same condition of obedience and worship. Then there is the emphasis in Ezekiel's proclamation of the new covenant that, as a result of God's dealings with Israel, they too "will know that I am the LORD" (Ezek. 34:27). Isaiah also speaks of the servant of the Lord as being a "covenant for the people" (42:6; 49:8), an expression the implications of which are not immediately evident, but its close association in 42:8 with the expression "a light for the Gentiles" leaves expanding implications. Then, in 42:4 not just Israel but the nations are portrayed as waiting for this servant to bring them God's law, and in 49:6 the LORD says, "It is too small a thing for you to be my servant to restore the tribes of Jacob and bring back those of Israel I have kept. I will also make you a light for the Gentiles, that you may bring my salvation to the ends of the earth." All these in their original contexts are little more than hints, but in retrospect at least, it is clear that God understood all along that this covenant would embrace his people the world over.

However, while questions remain in reference to any eschatological implications and in reference to the "mystery" aspect of this age of Gentile blessing *apart from* Israel (except for her small remnant), what is clear is that this new covenant community is indeed a new community. That is what Paul says of it in Ephesians 2:15: we who were far off and with no covenantal entitlements whatsoever have been brought near. But we have not simply been made Israel—the law's dividing wall has been abolished, and "one new man" has been created.

Jeremiah hints at this idea of the newness of the new covenant community as he introduces his prophecy with the words of a bitter proverb that evidently was commonly known in his day.

> *In those days they shall say no more, "The fathers have eaten sour grapes, and the children's teeth are set on edge." But every one will die for his own sin; whoever eats sour grapes—his own teeth will be set on edge* (Jer. 31:29-30).

This proverb presumably reflects a certain cynicism on the part of the people of Israel who complained of their suffering because of the unfaithfulness of their leaders. Under that old covenant God dealt with his people in what D.A. Carson describes as a "tribal" fashion.[12] One has only

---

[12] D. A. Carson, *Showing the Spirit* (Grand Rapids: Baker Academic, 1996), p. 152; "'You Have No Need That Anyone Should Teach You' (1 John 2:27): An Old Testament Allusion that Determines the Interpretation," in *The New Testament in Its First Century Setting: Essays on Context and Background in Honour of B. W. Winter on His 65th Birthday*, P. J. Williams, Andrew D. Clarke, Peter M. Head, and David Instone-Brewer, eds. (Grand Rapids: Eerdmans, 2004), pp. 277-9; "Evangelicals, Ecumenism, and the Church," in *Evangelical Affirma-*

to think of the various sufferings of the children of Israel that came to them under the old covenant because of the disobedience of their leaders. The focus of the complaint concerns individual responsibility, and Jeremiah announces that under this new covenant the old representative norms will be no more. Under this new arrangement God will deal with his people on an individual basis. The knowledge of God will no longer be mediated.

It is tempting to see in this cynical proverb and the way it is used a complete repudiation of the Reformed paedo-baptist view of the inclusion of believers' children in the covenant. Its emphasis that in the new covenant relationship with God will be a matter of individual experience may well be ground for saying so. But its focus is on the unmediated knowledge of God that will be enjoyed in the new covenant. This is perhaps a separate issue, so I am not quite convinced that we can push verses 29-30 quite that far.

It is beyond question, however, that this *is* the point of the following verses. God is promising a time in which *all* his covenant people will enjoy *all* of the covenanted blessings. The blessings of the covenant are co-extensive with the covenant community itself. Everyone in this community from the least to the greatest enjoys the privilege of sins forgiven, renewal and moral transformation, and the salvific knowledge of God. The old covenant community was a mixed community at its very best and was set aside, having failed to live up to its covenantal obligations. Not

---

tions, Kenneth S. Kantzer and Carl F. H. Henry, eds. (Grand Rapids: Zondervan, 1990), pp. 359-61.

God's law but sin itself was indelibly inscribed on Israel's heart (Jer. 17:1). But on just this score the new covenant community differs and enjoys higher privileges—her transgressions are forgiven; having been inwardly renewed she will be brought inevitably to perfect conformity to her covenantal obligations; all her people savingly know God and are indwelt by God's Spirit; and her full realization of all her covenantal blessings is guaranteed and secured in the blood of Christ. She is a qualitatively new community, a community of the redeemed. She is a perseveringly faithful community who, with sins forgiven, knows and walks in fellowship with God. She may not yet enjoy all of her promised blessings in full, but she is nonetheless a redeemed people and has been brought already to share in that fullness to come.

In a similar vein the writer to the Hebrews describes the new covenant community today as an outpost of the finally redeemed community in joyful assembly in heaven (Heb. 12:18-24). The old community dared never approach God but stood off in terror. But the church approaches with joyful boldness, having been brought near by the mediator of the new covenant, Jesus Christ, whose blood speaks better words than that of Abel. Everywhere, the New Testament writers insist that the church, this new covenant community, consists entirely of believers who in degree have already reached their final goal. This is no mixed assembly but a community of the redeemed. The new covenant forms a new community.

This distinctive is so pronounced in virtually all the new covenant passages that we Baptists are genuinely puzzled in wonder why others would extend the covenant sign to unbelieving children and thereby stretch the new covenant (as far as they are able) beyond its stated and promised bounds. We wonder in the first place on what exegetical ground our Reformed paedobaptist brothers can affirm the idea of covenants being made with believers and their children. There was a covenant with Abraham and _his_ descendants, but we know of no covenant made with _believers_ and _their_ children. And even if we did know of such a covenant, this is not it. This covenant forms a believing community and embraces the faithful only.

Central to this discussion is the promise that the new covenant community will be a Spirit-indwelt community— a people who from the least to the greatest of them know the empowering ministry of the Spirit of God. This theme looms large in Ezekiel's new covenant prophecy and throughout the New Testament with the repeated description of this age as the age of the Spirit and the many passages that speak, whether by way of anticipation or realization, of the powerful effects of the Spirit in the life of every believer. A blessing secured for every new covenant believer by the blood of Christ, the Spirit of God comes to minister to us and in us to accomplish all that is promised to us and required of us. Moses could only wish that all of God's people knew this Spirit of prophecy (Num. 11:29). Joel could only announce that such a day was coming (Joel 2:28-32). Then there was the promise of Messiah who would baptize not with water but with the Holy Spirit (Matt. 3:11; Mark 1:8; Luke 3:16; John 1:33). Then there was Christ's own promise of the "other helper" to come (John 14:16, 26; 15:26; 16:7; cf. 7:37-39) and his instruction to his disciples to wait in Jerusalem for the fulfillment of this promise (Acts

1:4-5). Then there was Pentecost, and the Spirit-empowered church was born. All through the book of Acts and the Epistles we read of the glorious fullness of the Spirit's great work in God's people in this age. The apostle Paul says we "read" the very same thing in the transformed life of every child of God in this age (2 Cor. 3:1ff). This is the mark of this new community. No longer is the knowledge of God mediated through representative leaders urging us to know the Lord. We all know him, personally and intimately, by his Spirit given to indwell us. This is not simply a new age but a new community, a new relationship between God and his people grounded in a new covenant promising and securing this very thing. In terms of our own experience all this hinges on God's gift of his Spirit.

Of course, this issue is notorious for its difficulty in allowing precise definitions of the work of the Spirit in the new covenant age as contrasted with that of the old covenant age. What is clear on the one hand is that the anticipation of the advent of the Spirit is massive and brimming with the expectation of a new and powerful work in God's people. Ezekiel promises it as a unique new covenant blessing. Jesus speaks similarly in John 7:37-39—"On the last and greatest day of the Feast, Jesus stood and said in a loud voice, 'If anyone is thirsty, let him come to me and drink. Whoever believes in me, as the Scripture has said, streams of living water will flow from within him.'" To this John adds the interpretive comment, "By this he meant the Spirit, whom those who believed in him were later to receive. Up to that time the Spirit had not been given, since Jesus had not yet been glorified." In Acts 1:8 he speaks again with similar anticipation: "You will receive power after the

Holy Spirit has come upon you." As we have already mentioned, this was the prophecy of John the Baptist, that Christ would baptize his people with the Holy Spirit. All this shouts with the expectation of a markedly new ministry of the Spirit in this new covenant age. And of course Luke leads us to see this expectation realized in Acts 2 when the Spirit descends upon the church at the day of Pentecost.

What confuses us is that, on the other hand, so many of the works of the Spirit highlighted in the New Testament seem evident also in the Old even if only at times and in degree. That the Spirit gave life-enabling faith seems a justified assumption for David, for example, whose heart was passionate in his pursuit of God. And we know of no other explanation for his love for God's law than the Spirit's transforming work. Whatever our explanation of these, we read of the Spirit working before Pentecost _in_ certain old covenant believers (_Joshua_: Num. 27:18, Deut. 34:9; _Ezekiel_: Ezek.2:2, 3:24; _Daniel_: Dan. 4:8-9, 18; 5:11; _Micah_: Mic. 3:8) and even of his "filling" them (_John the Baptist:_ Luke 1:15; _Elizabeth:_ Luke 1:41; _Zechariah:_ Luke 1:67).

Even so, a noticeable difference is evident. The Old Testament passages that speak of a work of the Holy Spirit under the Old Covenant, grand as they are in themselves considered, strike us as exceptional. Old Testament depictions of the Spirit of God coming upon someone to enable him for a given task and then leaving him again all seem out of place from a New Testament perspective. The Spirit's work in the Old Testament seems to us, comparatively, as rather _external, selective, temporary, task-oriented, and carefully measured._ His work then was certainly not as recognized, and it strikes us as falling considerably short of his new covenant ministry both in degree and in kind. In fact, the new covenant prophecies themselves leave us with this sense of contrast and anticipation. How, then, do we describe the difference between the Spirit's work in the Old and the New Testaments?

Doubtless the first step to answer this puzzle is to note that this blessing of the Spirit is never provided in the terms of the old covenant. It follows, then, that under the old covenant the Spirit's work was manifestly selective and not community wide. It is not clear what every member of the old covenant community even knew of the ministry of the Spirit, but what is clear is that ministry was not extended to every member of that community. This is likely the most radical difference. In this present age, Moses' wish (Num. 11:29) and Joel's prophecy (Joel 2:28-29) are realized—*all* God's people enjoy the great ministries of the Spirit to them and in them. This is the promise to every member of the new covenant community.

However, after even a cursory reading of the Old Testament passages that speak of the Spirit's ministry in that age, we sense from this new covenant perspective a stark difference not only in degree of teaching on the subject but in terms of our own experience. A quick highlighting of the Spirit's ministries in this age easily makes the point. The world-wide extension of the Spirit's convicting ministry in drawing the world to faith in Christ is a prominent emphasis of our Lord's in John 15:26-16:11. In 2 Corinthians 3 Paul describes the Spirit as having a work of illumination, renewal, and transformation in us in this age that the old covenant could never provide. In Acts, Luke graphically portrays the Spirit powerfully at work enabling the people of Christ to speak the word of God with boldness and with effective clarity. Beyond all this are the many passages that speak of the Spirit enabling and empowering us for service and, more significantly, "leading" and directing our wills to do his will, cleansing and purifying us, producing in us the many and deep graces of inward and outward righteousness he demands of us. Still more significant for us is his inciting in us a love for God, a love for his Word, and love for and unity with one another. Even more remarkable is his assuring us that our sins are gone, his assuring us of our sonship, his shedding abroad in our hearts a lively and instinctive awareness of God's fatherly love for us, making us feel and know experientially that we are his children. Still further, he strengthens us by cultivating in us an ever-increasing understanding of the incomprehensible love of Christ for us. As the firstfruit of the fuller harvest to come he inflames within us a hope and anticipation of the glory to which we have been destined. All this the Spirit does for _all_ who are in this new covenant, continuously and forever.

Just highlighting these many wonderful aspects of the Spirit's ministry in this age leaves us with the impression that it would stagger the old covenant believer and leave him breathless. Certainly from our perspective and experience, to revert back would for us be an immeasurable loss that would leave us reeling with a sense of lost helplessness. The very least among us has realized a ministry of the Spirit that is powerfully evident and that far outstrips the experience of the old covenant believer. Our knowledge of God mediated by Christ through his Spirit is greater and more intimate even than that of John the Baptist, the greatest of all who lived before us. Whatever frustrations mark the attempt to provide precise definitions in this regard, the comparison is telling. This is the age of the Spirit indeed.

The promise was that God would come and dwell with his people. The incarnation was God's first answer to that promise. Then there was Pentecost, the coming of the Spirit, whose "firstfruit" presence marks us off not only as a new redeemed community with a new experience but specifically as an outpost of the glorious heavenly community of the *eschaton*. That sense of expectation built into such passages as Ezekiel 36, Joel 2, John 7 and 14, and Acts 1:4-8 was not misleading. The sense of a new day of the Spirit evident in passages such as Acts, Romans 8:3-4, and 2 Corinthians 3 reflect a genuinely new reality and experience, one of which the older community could scarcely have imagined. In short, he has come to do what the law could not do—give life, a heart for God, obedience, assurance, perseverance, and certainty of hope. And this he does for all who are his—the entire new covenant community.

Again, to think—this is just the firstfruit, only the first installment. Oh, if this is just the firstfruit of the Spirit, what will his fullness be like in the day when our Lord comes to perfect this work in us? Words fail us. But that is to be expected, for at this point words failed the inspired apostle John also—"Beloved, it does not yet appear what we shall be, but we know that when he shall appear we shall be like him, for we shall see him as he is."

And so we conclude as we did our first lecture—with the distinctive cry of the whole church, "Come quickly, Lord Jesus!"

Summary

The new covenant promises soteric blessings that are inaugurated today in the church and that will be realized in fullness in the eschaton. New covenant theology seeks to follow the necessary and stated implications of this in recognition of the significant advance that marks this new covenant age brought about in Christ. These implications concern basic issues regarding how we are to read and understand our Bibles, the law of Moses and the new orientation of new covenant believers, the status and relevance of certain laws given in the old covenant (e.g., Sabbath), the nature of the covenants, and the nature and corresponding experience of their respective communities. This understanding leaves us—believers this side of the cross, this side of the resurrection, and this side of the ascension and Pentecost—with both a profound sense of blessing and privilege and an anticipation of still greater blessings and privileges ahead.

Made in the USA
Lexington, KY
21 March 2011